Beneath the Waves

Lily Murray

illustrated by Helen Ahpornsiri

For the Holters of Coast Road, Pevensey Bay
H. A.

First U.S. edition 2020
First published by Big Picture Press, an imprint of Bonnier Books U.K. 2019

Library of Congress Catalog Card Number pending
ISBN 978-1-5362-1040-8

20 21 22 23 24 25 TWP 10 9 8 7 6 5 4 3 2 1

Printed in Johor Bahru, Malaysia

This book was typeset in Garton, Perpetua, and Aristelle Script.
The illustrations were created with marine algae, petals, and leaves.

BIG PICTURE PRESS
an imprint of
Candlewick Press
99 Dover Street
Somerville, Massachusetts 02144

www.candlewick.com

Beneath the Waves

Lily Murray

illustrated by Helen Ahpornsiri

BPP

Contents

COAST

OPEN OCEAN

TROPICS

POLAR WATERS

Introduction

Hidden beneath the waves is another world.
In underwater cities of coral, schools of fish flash their
iridescent scales while great whales sing to one another across
the vast expanse of the open ocean. Dive deeper,
and on the seabed you'll find alien-looking creatures beyond
your wildest imaginings.

Each chapter of this book explores a different
ocean realm, brought to life with hand-pressed seaweed
and coastal plants. The tide pool is fringed with sea lettuce;
blades of bead weed circle the eye of the squid, while coral weed
paints the anglerfish a pale pink.
Fronds, stems, and petals are all transformed into the
wondrous creatures that live in the world's oceans.

Coast

Where the land meets the sea, the landscape
is constantly changing, reshaped by wind and
waves and the ebb and flow of the tide. From rocky shores
to muddy estuaries, sand dunes to salt marshes, coastal
habitats are incredibly rich in life. You can watch seabirds
soaring on the wind, search for porpoises playing in the
shallows, or explore the fascinating miniature world of a
tide pool.

With their clownlike faces, puffins are easy to spot as they gather on cliff tops to breed. In winter, their bills turn a dull gray.

Birds of the Sea

All along the coast, the air is filled with the sound of cawing gulls, swooping and diving on the wind. Far below them, wading birds run nimbly along the water's edge. They dance to and fro with the foaming waves, sometimes stopping to probe the sand for shellfish with their long beaks.

Many seabirds live far out in the open ocean and only come to the coast to breed. Each spring they flock to the cliffs, gathering in huge colonies known as seabird cities. Some, such as shags, perch on craggy outcrops, while others like gannets lay their eggs on narrow, rocky shelves. Puffins seek shelter from the elements, choosing to nest in abandoned rabbit burrows on the grassy cliff tops. When the last of the young have flown, the cliffs will fall silent — until spring comes again.

Gulls are masters of the air, able to fly and even hover in strong winds.

Seashells

Some seashells are pointed, while others are scalloped; there are seashells with twists and spirals, with rough edges and surfaces as smooth as pearls. All were once home to soft-bodied sea creatures known as mollusks.

Not all mollusks live in shells, but those that do keep their shells for life. They include thousands of different species, from oysters and mussels to limpets and snails. Thicker shells are better for protection, while lighter, smoother shells are more suited to moving quickly through the water.

Hunting for Homes

Some of the most intriguing creatures to spot along the shoreline are hermit crabs. Unlike other crabs, they don't grow protective shells, but make their homes inside the empty shells of other creatures.

As a hermit crab grows, its shell will become increasingly cramped until it has to move into a bigger one. When an empty shell washes ashore, numerous crabs will hurry to the scene. Remarkably, they line up by size and swap their shells, passing them down the line so that every crab gets a new home. If there aren't enough homes to go around, the crabs are prepared to put up a fight for them!

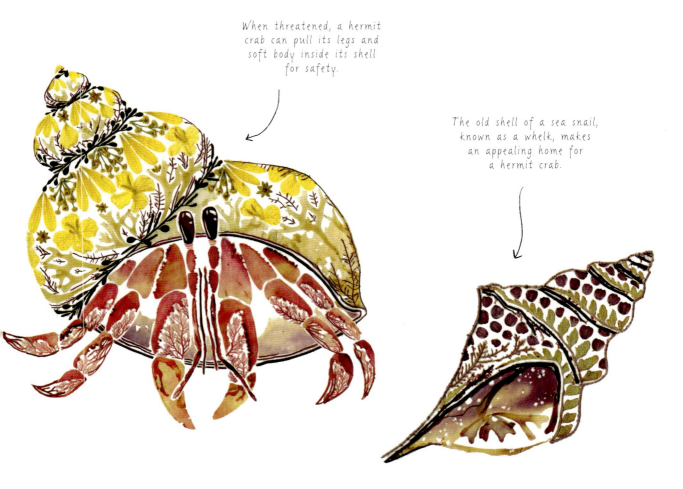

When threatened, a hermit crab can pull its legs and soft body inside its shell for safety.

The old shell of a sea snail, known as a whelk, makes an appealing home for a hermit crab.

In the Tide Pool

Tide pools only appear when the waves retreat and the tide goes out, revealing miniature underwater worlds.

The animals that live here have to cope with crashing waves, changing temperatures, and the risk of the tide pool evaporating under the hot sun and disappearing altogether. Conditions are rarely the same from one hour to the next. But despite all this, tide pools teem with life.

Related to jellyfish, sea anemones have stinging tentacles for catching prey.

Starfish cling to the rocks, crabs lurk in dark corners, and small fish dart between fronds of seaweed. At first glance, it may seem like an animal paradise, but look closer still, and you'll see life-and-death dramas playing out. Limpets battle against hungry starfish hunting for their next meal, and sea anemones fight one another for the best position in the pool while cuttlefish carefully sneak up on unsuspecting prey.

Star ascidians, also known as sea squirts, look like flowers but are actually jelly-like creatures. When disturbed, they expel jets of water.

Prawns move very quickly and can suddenly dart backward to avoid danger.

Seahorses are weak swimmers and anchor themselves to seaweed so they aren't swept away by strong currents.

The Seahorse

With their large eyes, arched necks, and long snouts, seahorses look like tiny horses. But despite appearances, these amazing creatures are members of the fish family.

Most seahorses live in shallow waters near the coast, tucked among corals and sea grasses. Courting couples dance together each morning, sometimes holding tails. Then the female passes her eggs to the male—he will carry them in a special pouch until they are ready to hatch.

Stars of the Sea

Starfish or sea stars have their own otherworldly beauty, with colorful arms radiating from a central body like the spokes on a bicycle wheel. From land, they can seem decorative and lifeless, but they are deadly predators.

Starfish move around slowly on tiny suction-cupped feet, which they also use to grip on to their hard-shelled prey, including mussels, clams, and snails. Once a starfish has made a catch, it pushes its sacklike stomach out of its mouth and inside the shell of its prey. There, the stomach envelops the prey's flesh and turns it into a souplike substance. The starfish then pulls its meal, and its stomach, back inside its body.

The spiny starfish grows slightly bigger than the size of your hand.

The common starfish usually ranges from orange to brown, but some can be deep violet.

Coast

Sea otters can dive down more than 300 feet/ 100 meters when foraging for food amid the kelp.

When diving, sea otters close their nostrils and ears to stop the water from getting in.

Forest Caretakers

Sea otters make their homes among vast forests of kelp, a type of giant seaweed that grows mainly in shallow waters along the coast.

The otters can be easily spotted at the surface, resting on their backs or sleeping peacefully on the rolling waves. Sometimes, they entangle themselves in the kelp so they aren't swept out to sea as they sleep.

Beneath the surface, the otters hunt for crabs, squid, octopuses, and sea urchins. Without the sea otters, these underwater forests would soon be destroyed by the sea urchins, which love to feast on the kelp.

Otters feed on crabs, clams, and sea urchins, using rocks as tools to break them open.

Tropics

Circling the middle of the Earth are the warm, crystal-clear seas of the tropics. Near the shore, young fish dart between the tangled roots of mangrove trees, while bright corals provide homes for some of the most bewitching creatures of the ocean. In the shallows, waving seagrasses form underwater meadows, grazed on by a whole host of species, from fish to turtles to slow-moving manatees.

The long spines of the
lionfish are highly venomous
for defense against attackers.
These fish are also fierce
predators of smaller fish.

Brightly colored butterfly fish peck at the reef with their long snouts, feeding on coral polyps, sea anemones, and worms.

Underwater Cities

Bright and colorful coral reefs are like bustling underwater cities. They are home to a quarter of all life in the oceans.

Reefs are living organisms made from the skeletons of tiny animals called coral polyps. For protection, polyps make hard outer cases for themselves out of minerals. When they die, they leave their cases behind and new polyps grow on top of them. Over time, coral reefs grow enormously. The largest is the Great Barrier Reef of Australia, which is 1,600 miles/ 2,600 kilometers long. The reefs provide shelter for a dazzling variety of creatures, including thousands of species yet to be discovered.

The blue-ringed octopus is covered in iridescent blue rings. These become brighter when the octopus feels threatened or is about to attack.

Deadly Beauty

Many animals on coral reefs are venomous, and the beautiful blue-ringed octopus is one of the deadliest of them all.

Although highly toxic, the octopus is small, measuring no more than 10 inches/ 25 centimeters across. It lives in shallow water and is a shy, elusive creature that hides in cracks and crevices in the reef, usually venturing out only at night to feed. Under cover of darkness, the octopus hunts fish and small crustaceans, grabbing prey in its tentacles, then killing it with a venomous bite. It can also release clouds of venom into the water to paralyze its prey.

Clownfish communicate with one another by making clicking and popping noises.

Home Sweet Home

Small striped clownfish live together among the waving tentacles of another reef creature — the sea anemone.

The anemone's tentacles are deadly to many fish, but clownfish have their own protection against its sting. A young clownfish will gently brush parts of its body against the anemone's tentacles. Over time, this enables the fish to build up a layer of mucus, which protects it from the anemone's stings.

The sea anemone provides the clownfish with food scraps, and its tentacles offer a refuge from predators. In return, the clownfish cleans the anemone, ridding it of parasites, and chases away butterfly fish that come to feed on the anemone.

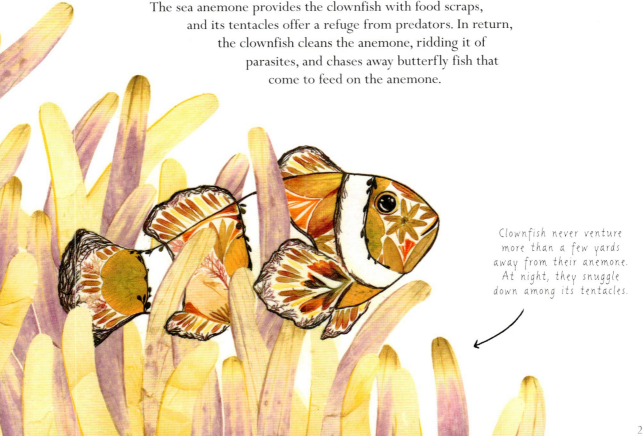

Clownfish never venture more than a few yards away from their anemone. At night, they snuggle down among its tentacles.

When they hatch, green turtles
are no bigger than a golf ball,
but as adults they will grow
up to 3½ feet/1 meter long.

Baby turtles travel long distances, floating in beds of seaweed near the ocean's surface.

Amazing Journeys

Swimming through the warm water comes a crowd of baby sea turtles. They have just survived a perilous journey down the beach where they hatched, past hungry crabs and gulls, into the welcoming waves of the sea.

Only two months before, the mother turtles arrived at the beach to lay their eggs. Each female dug a hole in the sand, filled it with eggs, and covered the hole before returning to the sea. Now that the hatchlings have made it to the ocean, they will drift for years on the currents, eating plankton, prawns, and small jellyfish. As they grow older, they will swim along the coast feeding on sea grasses. One day, the females will return to the beach where they were born and at last lay eggs of their own.

The golden-brown sea nettle's stinging tentacles paralyze, but do not kill, its prey.

Sea Nettle

A beautiful bell-shaped jellyfish, the sea nettle drifts on ocean currents, spreading its tentacles wide to catch its prey.

The sea nettle feeds on small fish, crustaceans, and tiny sea creatures called zooplankton. It catches prey in its stinging tentacles, then carries it up to its mouth. Although it prefers to drift, the sea nettle can move by sucking water into its body and then squirting it back out again. This way, it is able to migrate each day from the dark depths of the ocean to the sunlit surface above.

Sea Krait

A sea krait winds its way across the reef, its body sweeping smoothly through the clear water as it hunts for its favorite prey—eels.

Unlike other sea snakes, the sea krait will come ashore to mate and lay its eggs. It can creep across rocky islands and even climb trees, but is superbly suited to life in the sea. Large lungs mean it can stay underwater for up to two hours at a time, and its flattened tail works like a paddle, powering the snake through the water. When the sea krait finds prey, it strikes with deadly venom, swallowing eels whole.

Sea kraits hunt for prey among the nooks and crannies of a coral reef.

The banding on a sea krait warns would-be predators that it is highly venomous.

Winged Fish

Manta rays glide through tropical waters on their winglike fins, constantly moving to keep water flowing over their gills. Both gentle and curious, they are among the most intelligent species of fish.

Although they can reach up to 23 feet/7 meters across, manta rays feed on some of the smallest creatures of the ocean—zooplankton. They first slowly circle their prey, then swim through it with their mouths open wide before filtering the plankton through slits on either side of their throat. Manta rays also leap out of the water in acrobatic displays, possibly to communicate with one another, or maybe just for fun.

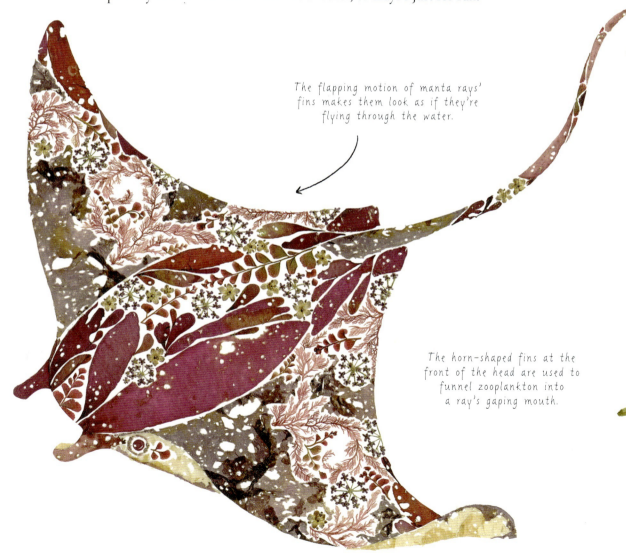

The flapping motion of manta rays' fins makes them look as if they're flying through the water.

The horn-shaped fins at the front of the head are used to funnel zooplankton into a ray's gaping mouth.

Strange Sharks

Hammerheads are unusual-looking, with their flattened heads and wide-spaced eyes.

Their heads are full of sensory organs that detect the electrical fields created by their prey. This is especially helpful when it comes to finding their favorite meal, stingrays, which like to hide in the sand.

By night, hammerheads hunt alone, but in the day they gather together in huge schools. These make a mesmerizing sight in summer as vast numbers of hammerheads set off in search of cooler waters.

Open Ocean

Far out to sea, beyond the coast, lies the vast expanse
of the open ocean. It covers more than
half of the Earth's surface, and its predators must
travel far and fast in their search for food — there
is much less to go around than in the shallow seas.
There are creatures here that spend their entire lives
surrounded by water on all sides, some never seeing
land or even sunlight.

Fast and Free

From dolphins to marlins to tuna, some of the fastest swimmers in the ocean inhabit its open waters. They often live in large groups, thousands strong, for protection against predators.

Schools of tuna can reach speeds of up to 43 miles/69 kilometers per hour, their silver scales flashing as they cover vast distances in search of food. To escape the tuna, flying fish have evolved torpedo-shaped bodies, enabling them to swim fast enough to break the surface of the water. Dolphins, too, reach great speeds as they hunt. They can leap from the water, twisting and turning before plunging beneath the waves.

Common dolphins are among the fastest of all marine mammals, reaching speeds of more than 25 miles/ 40 kilometers per hour.

By spreading their winglike fins, flying fish can glide for hundreds of yards over the ocean's surface.

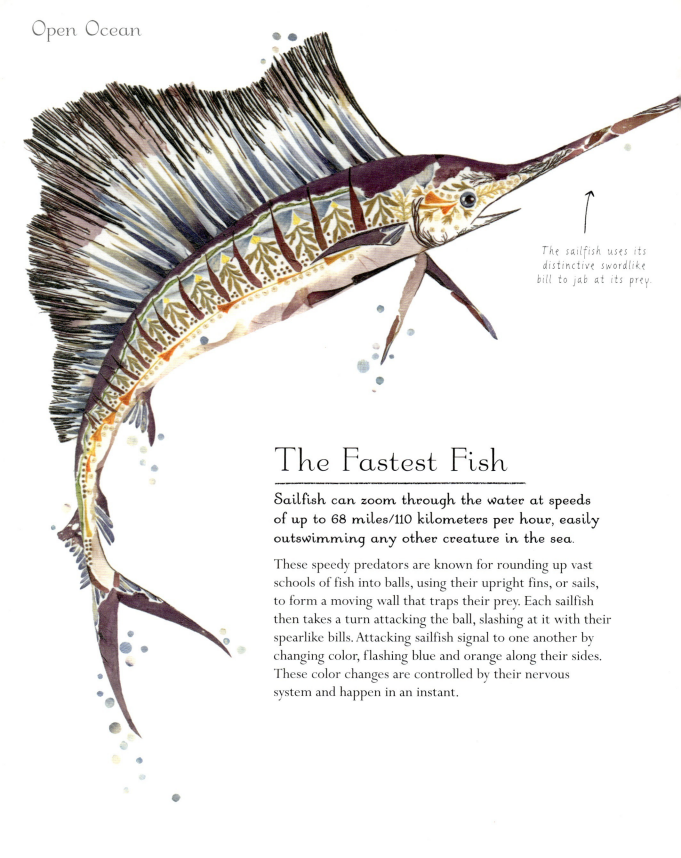

The sailfish uses its distinctive swordlike bill to jab at its prey.

The Fastest Fish

Sailfish can zoom through the water at speeds of up to 68 miles/110 kilometers per hour, easily outswimming any other creature in the sea.

These speedy predators are known for rounding up vast schools of fish into balls, using their upright fins, or sails, to form a moving wall that traps their prey. Each sailfish then takes a turn attacking the ball, slashing at it with their spearlike bills. Attacking sailfish signal to one another by changing color, flashing blue and orange along their sides. These color changes are controlled by their nervous system and happen in an instant.

Ocean Hunters

Blue sharks are curious creatures, famed for their long, elegant bodies and graceful swimming motion. However, they are also voracious predators.

Although they reach up to 10 feet / 3 meters long, blue sharks hunt surprisingly small prey, including sardines and cuttlefish. They will also eat anything they can find, stealing food from fishermen's nets or scavenging on dead whales.

Blue sharks are found in waters around the world. They are instantly recognizable by the bright-blue skin along the top of their bodies, while their underbellies are a ghostly white. This helps them to blend in with the water when seen from above and below.

Blue sharks are often surrounded by pilot fish, which eat parasites on the shark's scales and leftover scraps from its meals.

Mysterious Giants

The largest fish in the sea, whale sharks are as long as a bus. They feed by sucking in water through their giant gaping mouths and then filtering out tiny plants and animals.

Whale sharks swim slowly but will travel huge distances in search of food and are capable of diving to incredible depths. Despite their vast size, little is known about their lives. However, each whale shark has a unique pattern of spots and pale stripes, which helps researchers to identify individuals.

These fish are too big
to be prey for the whale
shark. Instead, they hitch
a ride in its wake as it
moves through the water.

Life in the Depths

The deep sea is dark, hostile, and largely unexplored. It is also the largest habitat in the ocean, greater in size than almost all the other ocean habitats put together.

The creatures down here are like nothing you have ever seen before. Many make their own light to attract prey and have large eyes for scanning the dark waters. They tend to migrate to the surface each night to feed and descend again to the depths by day. There are viperfish that snap up prey in their long, fanglike teeth; lanternfish with silvery scales; and, brightest of all, the firefly squid, whose whole body glows in the darkness like a blue star.

Every spring, in Toyama Bay in Japan, thousands of firefly squid come together, creating an amazing light display.

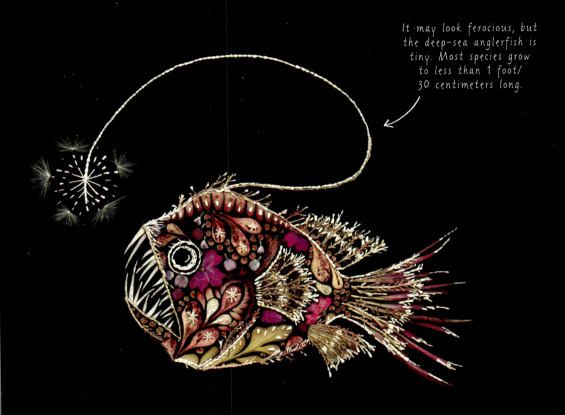

It may look ferocious, but the deep-sea anglerfish is tiny. Most species grow to less than 1 foot/ 30 centimeters long.

A Light in the Dark

The deeper you go in the ocean, the less light there is. Found at a depth of 3,000 feet/914 meters, the female anglerfish has a remarkable solution to finding prey — a light-tipped lure.

A piece of luminous flesh hangs at the end of the anglerfish's spine, and she uses it like a fishing rod to attract prey in the dark. Her backward-curving teeth help to trap her victims before she gulps them down. She is able to stretch her stomach to accommodate creatures up to twice her size.

The males are much smaller than females. When young, they will latch on to a female with their sharp teeth. Over time, their bodies fuse together, and the male will feed from the female like a parasite.

A giant squid's eyes are
the size of dinner plates
and help it detect prey
in the gloomy depths.

44

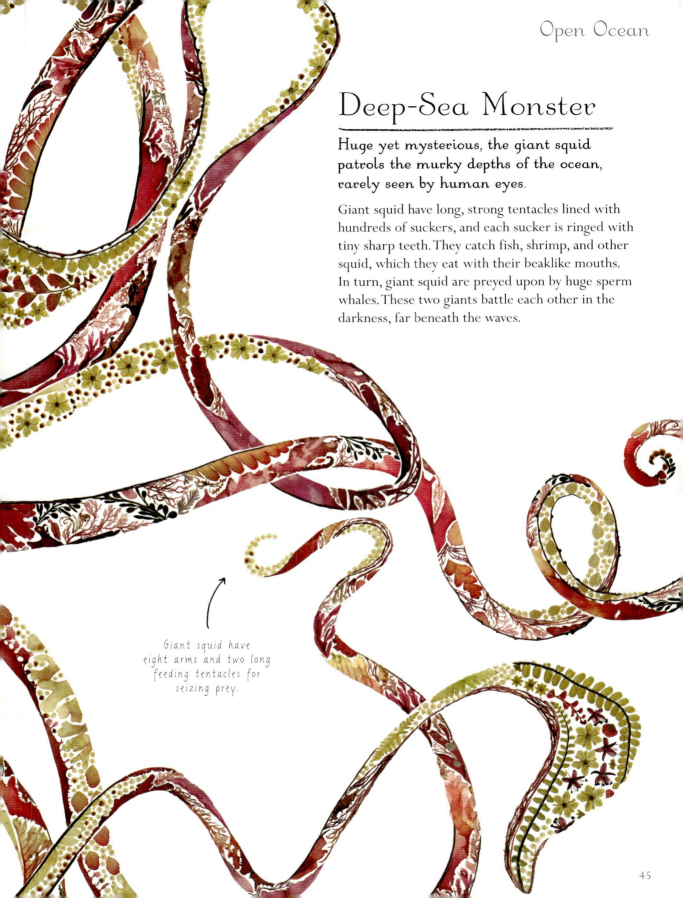

Deep-Sea Monster

Huge yet mysterious, the giant squid patrols the murky depths of the ocean, rarely seen by human eyes.

Giant squid have long, strong tentacles lined with hundreds of suckers, and each sucker is ringed with tiny sharp teeth. They catch fish, shrimp, and other squid, which they eat with their beaklike mouths. In turn, giant squid are preyed upon by huge sperm whales. These two giants battle each other in the darkness, far beneath the waves.

Giant squid have eight arms and two long feeding tentacles for seizing prey.

Polar Waters

At the very top and bottom of the world lie the north and south poles. It is cold all year and much of the water is frozen in sheets of thick white ice. Despite freezing temperatures, there is a huge abundance of life. The waters are full of plankton and krill, which attract vast schools of fish, migrating whales, flocks of seabirds, and huge colonies of seals.

Waddle and Wait

It is April in Antarctica: the sea ice has thickened and thousands of emperor penguins have come inland to breed. Each penguin has a thick layer of fat and closely packed feathers, but in the bitter cold they must huddle together for warmth.

The females each lay a single egg, then return to the sea to hunt, leaving the males to care for the eggs. For the females it is a long journey of up to 50 miles/ 80 kilometers. But for the males, it is a tough two-month wait through the winter.

On the female's return, both parents take turns looking after their chick. They waddle and toboggan to the ocean and back to meet its demands for food. By December, the chick is finally old enough to swim and fish. At last, it can leave the frozen wastes of sea ice and take to the water with its parents.

By September, the chicks
are covered in a thick layer
of down. They are quickly
growing and always hungry.

Emperor penguins are the
largest species of penguin,
growing to around the height
of a six-year-old child.

Wandering albatrosses
have been known to travel
thousands of miles over
several days.

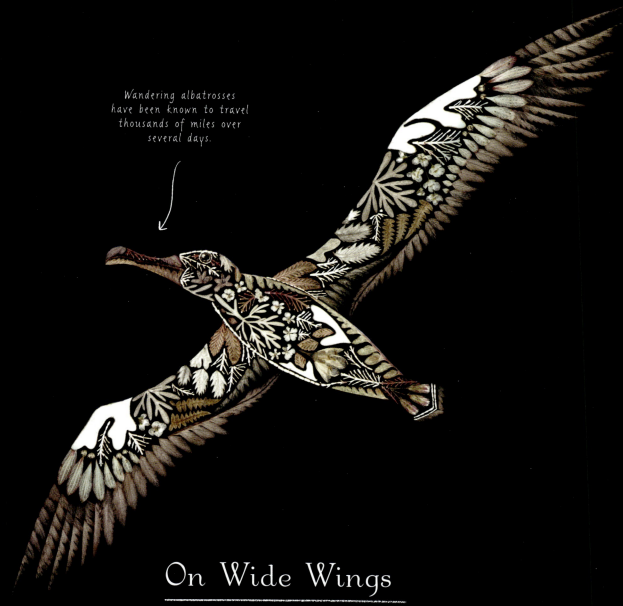

On Wide Wings

Soaring across the waters of the Southern Ocean, the wandering albatross has the largest wingspan of any bird, more than 10 feet/3 meters from tip to tip.

These feathered giants will glide for hours on their outstretched wings. In just a few days, they can travel from their breeding grounds near Antarctica as far as the seas off Uruguay and back again. At night, they will sometimes roost on the surface of the sea, but they spend most of their lives on the wing. Sailors often told stories about these majestic birds, known to follow fishing boats in the hope of a meal.

Seals and Walruses

In the frozen waters of the Arctic, seals, whales, and walruses cruise the chilly ocean. They feed on fish, shellfish, and crustaceans such as krill and are kept warm by their thick layers of fatty blubber.

Harp seals are known for their fluffy white young, called pups, which are born on the ice. Mothers can identify their pups from hundreds of others by scent alone. Walruses also come onto the ice to breed. Mustached and tusked, they bellow and snort, and males are aggressive during mating season. But mothers are incredibly tender with their young, often cradling them in their flippers.

The long grooves lining a blue whale's throat expand so the whale can take in huge mouthfuls when feeding.

Ocean Giants

Blue whales are the biggest animals ever to have lived. Their tongues alone weigh as much as an adult elephant!

Remarkably, blue whales feed on tiny, shrimplike krill, taking in huge mouthfuls at a time. Each summer, their search for food takes them from the warm waters of the equator to the cooler waters of the poles, where krill live in abundance. When traveling alone, whales stay in constant contact — their deep, rumbling calls carry vast distances underwater.

Blue whales swallow huge mouthfuls of water and krill. Then they push the water out through the bristles that line their mouths and swallow the krill that are left behind.

Male narwhals cross tusks, perhaps to impress females.

Unicorns of the Sea

Known as "unicorns of the sea" for their single white tusks, narwhals live only in Arctic waters.

These mysterious creatures are cousins of dolphins and porpoises. They live in small groups, gliding under sea ice before bobbing up for air. The narwhal's tusk was once thought to have magical powers and was worth more than gold. We now know it to be a long, spiralling tooth, usually found only in males. It grows up to 10 feet / 3 meters long and has thousands of nerve endings. A narwhal will use its tusk to impress rivals, stun fish, and sense its surroundings in the murky polar waters.

King of the Ice

Polar bears are the world's largest meat-eating land animal. But their Latin name, *Ursus maritimus*, means "sea bear," and they spend most of their lives on the sea ice.

To survive in the freezing Arctic, polar bears have a dense white fur coat, a thick layer of body fat, and black skin to soak up the sun's rays. They are masters of their environment — skilled hunters with no natural enemies. On padded paws, they will creep up on sleeping seals or wait for hours by a hole in the ice for a seal to come up to breathe. They are also powerful swimmers, capable of paddling more than 400 miles / 600 kilometers between ice floes in search of their next meal.

Polar bears mainly feed on seals and other fatty animals, but will sometimes eat berries or even chase fish.

Recognizable by their tall dorsal fins and black-and-white markings, orcas are the largest members of the dolphin family.

Powerful Predators

They surge through the waves, their bodies sleek and glistening, one of the most powerful hunters of the ocean. But orcas, also known as killer whales, are more than just predators. They live in close-knit family groups that stay together for generations.

Orca groups, or pods, are led by an older female, usually a grandmother or great-grandmother. Each pod has its own food preferences, such as a particular species of fish or seal, as well as its own calls. Hunting techniques are passed down from one generation to the next, and a pod will work together to care for young or sick members of its group. Mothers will stay in touch with their offspring for life.

A Note from the Artist

The art in this book is all made from seaweed, coastal flowers, and a few garden plants, collected and pressed after a series of trips to the shore.

Submerged, seaweeds reveal the most graceful shapes, but when removed from the water, many become indistinguishable clumps. This makes pressing them a challenge. Specimens must be floated, then slowly raised out of the water on sheets of paper. Only then can they be preserved and arranged: fronds of purple laver cut to create the patterns on a whale shark, and calcified fronds of common coral weed used to outline deep-sea creatures.

The seaweed used in this book was collected along the south coast of England — found in clumps on the shoreline after a storm, or left behind during low tide. Care was taken not to remove any seaweed from its holdfast and to cause as little disturbance to the environment as possible.

Glossary

breeding: when animals produce young or offspring

colony: a large group of animals living together

crustacean: an animal with a hard shell and several pairs of legs that usually lives in water

fish: a cold-blooded animal with a backbone. Most fish have jaws, gills, and fins. Sharks and rays are types of fish.

gill: the organ through which most fish and sea creatures absorb oxygen from the water

mammal: a warm-blooded animal that feeds its young with milk. Mammals are usually covered with fur or hair and give birth to live young.

migration: the movement of animals from one place to another, over a long distance, to look for food or better surroundings

mollusk: an animal with a soft body, often covered by a shell. Many mollusks live in water.

organism: a living thing

parasite: an organism that lives off another organism and gives nothing in return

predator: an animal that hunts and eats other animals

school: a huge group of fish

shark: a long-bodied fish that hunts its prey. Sharks have skeletons made from cartilage and large, stiff fins.

tentacle: a long, thin body part used for feeding or grasping prey

tide: the rise and fall of the sea that happens twice a day

whale: a large sea mammal with a long body, flippers, and a horizontal tail fin

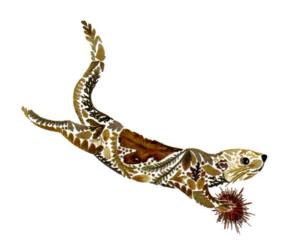